EMBARKATION
FOR
CYTHERA

a cycle of poems by
Iain Hamilton

with a prefatory note
by
Sir John Betjeman

Martin Brian *&* O'Keeffe Limited,
London 1974

ISBN 0 85616 350 3

Designed and printed in London at The Curwen Press

For Jean, with love

The one way to get
To the land of Et-Et
Is round and about
Through the maze of Aut-Aut.

Gaiety transfiguring all that dread
W. B. Yeats

CONTENTS

ACKNOWLEDGMENTS

Many of the poems in this cycle have appeared elsewhere in more primitive form. Some have been broadcast. Acknowledgments are due to Adam, the British Broadcasting Corporation, Wm Collins and Sons, the Glasgow Herald, the Guardian, Longmans Green, Public Opinion, the Scots Review, the Spectator, the Student of Edinburgh University, the Times Educational Supplement, and the Times Literary Supplement.

I owe much to many for their friendship and candour, but here I should like to acknowledge with warmest gratitude my especial indebtedness to a pair of learned friends whose hawk-eyes helped my own blurred vision to recognize some infelicities: the many that remain do so against the better judgment of Brendan Kennelly and Thomas Treadwell.

This is number

of a limited edition
of fifty copies

PREFACE

Sir John Betjeman

A Sheáin, sheán-chara dhílis:
Tá áthas orm mar gheall ort—

which, as you know, in rough translation into the Bearla
may be rendered as:

Oh, Iain, my old and faithful friend:
There is joy in me because of you

I like your poems: They are Scottish and gritty and
Glaswegian. You have an eye for landscape and an ear
for rhythm and rhyme — and a heart.

Is mise le meas mór,

Seán O'B

PROLOGUE

Out of the north

Green flecked with blond, and
blackthorn. Raw red brick
of railroad buildings.
Farther, toybox lines
of fuming steelworks.
Beyond them, sprinkled
hill-after-hill and
powder sky and clouds
like pussmoths whirring
over slagheaps, and
prim rows of dwellings
with crossed antennae—
there, where sulphur thins,
breaks down, disperses
under the brassy
sun that blares out bold
from coast to coast, blasts
clean out from peering
travellers' fretting wits
their sour anxieties
and rolls them bowling
over the lea from
Tinto top to Pent-
land ridge, the loco-
motive moaning on
to Beattock, purring
on into evening,
drumming over Esk,
while travellers, musing,
see in stain of cloth
or slop of glass those
lines of fuming works

1

beyond the raw red
brick of railroad shacks,
green, and blackthorn, green,
green, green flecked with blond.

Scream of steam and steely whine
Free him from winter's frozen clutches,
Shoot him into a future showering
Flower and fruit, the sun's bright riches,
Rattle him out
Of the iron north
From biting winds and words that he
Had learned to take for granted.

Apple, cherry, almond, pear
Foam on the rolling curves of green.
With greedy eyes he guzzles each
And every dappled passing scene—
Nouveau riche
In the sun's bright bounty,
Parvenu planted in plenty, how
Can he take this for granted?

Sun demands no heartbreak fee
For lavish labour of light and heat:
Old news this, but gawkily
He stands and stares where seasons meet
And merge and mask
Themselves with the rainbow.
No one here, rich or poor,
But takes it all for granted.

Scraps of letters penned in pain
From shattered city, ripped plain,
Persuade him that another sun
May rise to zenith and remain,
Reason its radiance,
Oneness its warmth,

Till at length and at last we all may
Take its wealth for granted.

Doors may then lie open and
Men walk easy in the sun,
Stretch their arms and never fear
The dull grenade, the gaping gun,
Wear smiles neither
Forced nor frozen,
Move like aristocrats among their riches,
Taking them all for granted.

I: BY THE DARK SHORE

The shrill cicalas, single-stringed,
Announce the entrance of the night,
And by their pine-tree on the cliff
I watch the shot-silk water's light
Grow cold and glassy as the day's
Last finger slides away from sight.
The islands in the bay's embrace
Dissolve, are lost; and now alone
Above the swaying waves that play
Bleak elegies on sand and stone,
I swing within a colder tide—
The grief that flows from blood and bone.

Numbly I stare into the night
That trembles to the convent bell
Ringing for Christ across the bay.
The dark is singing like a shell
When clean across the vacancy
There sweeps the urgent light of Cap Fréhel.

News of the world

As I came round by Templeton's
The sun was sliding low,
And every spire round Glasgow Green
Gave off its godly glow.

Deep in its rut the river shed
A skin of shit and scum,
And glinted through the fretted bridge,
Gold as Byzantium.

Then suddenly the sun was snuffed
Behind a sooty cloud,

And night let fall on Glasgow Green
Its sulphur-stinking shroud.

Black in its bed the river slinks
Down to the whining weir.
The yellow lamps along its banks
Come out—and with them, fear.
And fear floods out and fills the dark,
And the dark and the fear are one,
And standing on this bridge I know
The things that must be done.

For hardly fifty yards from here
Last night at half-past-ten
A Southside girl was gagged and shagged
By seven Brigton men.
And when the bully-boys were done,
They left her on the mud:
A crumpled stem and a crushed flower
And a dark splash of blood.

The slimy river secretly
Slid on, and far away
A furnace flared into the night
And the night was light as day.
A whistle shrilled. Across the Green
To London Road the men
Ran stumbling, and to hide their flight
The darkness dropped again.

But torchlight sliced the darkness where
She lay limp on the mud.
A crushed flower and a crumpled stem
And a dark splash of blood.
And torchlight fell on the twisted face
And it fell on the tangled hair.
On the clawed thighs, on the clenched fists
The torches threw their glare.
And then big Seán of Surrey Street
Came knifelike through the crowd,

And when he knew that it was true
He swore by holy blood
That he would hunt the bastards down
Had dibbled dirty seed,
And all their cheeks would grin like lips
And every throat would bleed.

Aye, well might the stinking river sink
As though in fear it fell.
And well might the rising sun burn red
As though it rose on hell.
For thirteen Southside men had sworn
To smear their blades with blood
For the crumpled stem and the crushed flower
And the red stain on the mud.

And now as I stand on the swaying bridge
Above the sluggish stream,
I know that a night of knives is down
And I know it is no dream.
My fingers clutch the greasy rail,
Frozen fast by fear.
A minute from the clanging street,
And yet I cannot stir.
And faint and far across the Green
To the grimy banks of Clyde
From the depth of the dark there twists a scream
Like a slow sword in the side.
Cry upon cry, and the crying rises,
Falls, and swells again,
And nearer, louder beat the drumming
Feet of running men,
Till close at hand the thud of feet
Is stilled. The shouting dies.
The furnace flares. The killing ground
Is framed beneath my eyes.

At the place on the path where it was done
Last night at half-past-ten,
Their blades ablaze like liquid light
Are seven Brigton men.

They stand like a glinting rock on the shore
As the tide creeps all around—
Thirteen crouching Southside men
Who move without a sound.

And they close on the men who stand on the spot
Where she lay sprawled on the mud.
A crumpled petal, a crushed stem,
And a dark splash of blood.

Is it only fear that holds me here
Where I stand on the bridge alone,
Though I know how a blade can slice as though
Through blubber to the bone?

A twisted face and tangled hair
And clawed thighs on the mud.
A crumpled stem and a crushed flower
And a dark splash of blood.

And a shaking scream from a broken boy
Is signal for the shock.
Cry upon cry. With a flashing surge
The sea is upon the rock.
A chalky face is crossed with red,
And again, again, again.
Behind the savage glitter of
A filed and flailing chain,
I see a boy go down on his back,
His muffler running red,
While the kid who killed him falls beside
Him, gashed across the head.

The furnace flames are curling low
And the dark returns at last,

And through the scream of fighting shrills
A piercing whistle blast.
And darkness drops on the Green again
And I move like a man in a dream—
A dream of hell—but knowing well
That things are what they seem.

Is there a man who never knew
A red mist mask his sight?
Is there a man who never knew
The joy I knew tonight?

As I came round by Templeton's
The sun was sliding low.
In a black night of black despair
From Glasgow Green I go.

II: TO THE INLAND SEA

That steady oar-stroke drives me on.

No longer shackled to the land,
In a dark galley proof against
All snags of rock and snares of sand,
I sail exultant through the night,
The tiller live beneath my hand,
Away from darkness into light.

The rocks of Finistère recede
And Biscay's heavy miles are gone:
And yet, for all this leaping speed,
Those dancing strokes that drive me on
Along the course my senses lead,
South and to certainty, even so
I trail the sickness of my kind,
I trawl the malaise of despair.
Like a tin to a tormented hound,
The butt of children's cruelty,
So my sea-anchor drags behind.

But coming up to anchorage
In a haven of the inland sea,
I'll cut this burden clean adrift
And see it sink and so renew
At a single stroke my innocence.

In passion alone is purity.

Old sun up there, now mounting Ida,
Ripping aside the shredded cloud,
Tear out of me awareness of
All things that cannot stir the blood
And drive it on with love or hate.

Burn out my sickness with a blazing flood!

Observers

Grown granite-hard, they stand in spite of buffets,
And eyes once mild have chilled to bleak precision,
Broken and bruised their power of transmuting
Bodies or bricks to glory through their vision.
And hearts without fuel must chill. Now none
Of them would turn his accurate head to see
Great Agamemnon poised to knife his daughter,
Or a limp saviour hanging from a tree.

III: LANDFALL

So Ulysses came home at last,
Tense as his bow and taut as its string,
His galley gone, his journey done.

Now noon, the cutting colours sing
Within the bounds so deeply drawn.
The sun that chisels everything
With fiery edge has carved away
The coat of flesh that clothed this bone,
And the island that I enter stands
As bare as the immortal skeleton,
With little left to fill or bridge
The clefts between unknown and known.

A scarf of sand that burns my feet,
A wall of rocks, deep-hollowed, worn,
A rank of dunes and stinging grass,
Beyond the shore a terrain torn
By black ravines, a slope of olives,
Over all a rocky horn.

And here's the homeland—no Cockayne!

No Watteau limned this paradise,
Bare of the blandishments that grow
In sleep before the inward eyes
Of those who free themselves in dreams
From urgencies of thought or thighs.

I skirt the cabins by the shore,
Shut tight against the mid-day sun,
And stumble on a stone as dogs
Come at me, snarling as they run.
No welcome here. I beat them off
And cripple a few before I've done.

Hah! how my stride is free and long,
How sure my step on stone and grass.
If a lout should try to stop me now
I'd brush him to the side and pass
As if the bruiser were no more
Than a blowfly on a looking-glass.

An elegiac air, on a theme of Oliver St John Gogarty's

('Till I am dead, and changed to air,
O walk not in the wind!')

Why do you pause? Why turn and move away,
Smoothing your skirt, your thought, your hair
At one endearment from my eager lips?
Because I take the trees
And where
The waves refuse me how
I crush their curling crests to spray?

But, ah, for you I have a different kiss.
No lover could caress you so
Enchantingly, awakening desire
To unmask mystery:
For know,
Sweet girl who turns away,
The sea our mother taught me this.

Mortal and vulnerable, turn and gaze
Upon the sea. My fingers touch
Your fine and flowing hair. Throw back your head.
I kiss your trembling neck.
And such
Sweet pain as this is all
The solace of my circling days.

I pause. Each pleat falls back into its fold,
Each thought, and you are as you were
Before I found you turning from the shore,
This shore to which I once
Brought her
Whom men will seek in you
And glimpse, and find, and fail to hold.

IV: AGAINST COUNTERFEITERS

Untrue!
       Recant!
              I reached the shore
Encumbered still. I had no knife.
Crossing the sand, I felt my fear
Awake at the lifting of a leaf
On the burning wind.
                Where was the guide
Into this new and naked life?

Swaddled and coddled and wrapped around
In metaphysical despair,
This figure of fun, this frowsy freak
Of a tragical-farcical northerner
Has a tongue grown stiff, for here it's clear
There's little use for metaphor.

I have come home to the world of things
To learn the imperative, 'Rejoice!'
But where's the good of mouthing it
If straining, draining through the voice
Come all the dismal echoes of
The arguments behind the choice?
How can I stir myself unless
This abstract load falls off my back,
This ragbag of absurdities?
And how rejoice without the knack
Of seeing straight and feeling straight
And speaking straight that still I lack?

To feel the earth fill out my flesh,
Lodged in my breast the livid sun,
A flower in every finger's end,
The tumbled rock inside my bone,
Sea and sap within my blood,

Cupped in my skull the gleaming moon—
And yet to know myself a part
Of all around, below, above
That all the senses can engage;
To feel the flux of hate and love
Flow without end yet be all end—
There's the philosophy I crave.
For safe in such a matrix I'd
Withstand whatever blows might fall;
And what if this knuckle-end were hammered
Down and stretched like a broken wall
If I knew that nothing ends, that nothing
Ceases to live that has lived at all!

Out-staring ruin I'd applaud
The latest scene in the endless play
Of death-in-life and life-in-death,
And like both poet and madman say:

'All things fall and are built again
And those that build them again are gay.'

Oh, easy words, confidence tricksters
Trotting out your stale deception,
Tripping us up at every turning,
Pimps assured of prompt reception,
Counterfeiters welcomed gladly,
Twisters of all true perception:
How do you help me here and now
To clear the eye and straighten the back
And quicken the blood and loosen the tongue
And get me off this crazy rack
And give me the wit and the will to quit
This scorching sand and find the track?

The track?

        To where?

                That flash—what is it,
There, in the gaps among the trees

On the hill?
             A movement.
                          Voices calling
My name are carried on the breeze.

Like sunsplit spray, that leaping laughter.
Shoulders, flanks, breasts, knees,
And tossing hair between the tree-trunks,
Coming and going, laughter playing,
Fountains dancing, leaves and water,
Out of the depths a green voice saying
My name, again and again, my name,
Like one half-jeering and half-praying.

High talk at Moy

The yellow light
that floods along the wall
and lifts a palm-spray into
black relief
buoys me from gloom
into a high belief
that should I rise and walk
across the hall
and towards you, all
the orchard-trees would bud
and blossom and bear, and all
in a second's space.

And knowing this,
I know that sudden grace
would quell the rage and riot
of our blood
and make us equal,
join us, make us one,
so we, being one, might have
no thought at all
of imperfection.

Yellow light
that floods along the wall,
you drown the urge to break
the pose and run.

V: THE TRUEST POETRY
IS THE MOST FEIGNING

When the painter turns away at last
From images he's found or made,
He may describe a glade unentered,
Games he's watched but hasn't played,
And limbs that never lay with his:
For these are staples of his trade;
And how should he say that here is life,
And there mere images of life?
The frozen picture melts and moves.
Pygmalion makes himself a wife.
Shadow and substance fly together.
Contraries conclude their strife.

And so at last the painter knows
What stirred in Adam as he stood
Knee-deep in clover and felt the wind
Caress the arms his blood had scarcely
Warmed,
      and gazed around,
               and knew
That all before his eyes was good.

And so he conjures up the boy
Stilled in a sudden dream, his eyes
New-misted by the love of love,
The force that makes the sap to rise,
The world transfigured and its sounds
Conjoined in melting harmonies.

Those crested promontories strain
At the limestone leash like lizards tethered,
Frantic for freedom, pulling seaward,
Africaward, their blind force gathered
Into one sullen brutish bulk
Of longing for a land that's weathered

Down to the bone, beyond it, ground
To flat infinities of death.

Yet they are beautiful.
                                    They live,
Merging in distance like a breath
In the morning air—

                                    those promontories
Of life, extremities of faith.

And am I kept from death like them
And held in life because of my
Last-ditch refusal to accept
Defeat from mere infinity
And its malignant myths which cry:
'How easy to lie down and die!'?

I am no bravo on the brink
To step breast-forward into space
And stretch myself in front of some
Ingenious ghoul with gorgon face
Engendered by myself, and so
Go down and out without a trace.

Above the hazed horizons rising,
Shades of dreams within the dream
That man must make and multiply
Until the empty quarters teem:
Poor figments—but with power to dowse
The single life-sustaining gleam.
And so they must not be denied,
The large chimeras and the least.
There's not a wisp that cannot turn
Itself into a tearing beast,
Like a medium's cheesecloth sprouting jaws
And having the faker for a feast.

And as they twist and turn, so I
Acknowledge all their hollow power
And honour every frenzied dance—

Then fix my eyes on this one flower
And give them not another glance;
For this is not their killing-hour;
This is the hour to celebrate
Clear depths above, dark depths below,
And then to move because I must,
So fiercely through my senses flow
The urgent signals from the hidden
World of wonders that I've feared to know.

A prothalamion

In Jura, cradled by the moonstruck sea,
Enwrapped and lapped by love's simplicity,
The day may seem an hour, the hour a minute:
May
The moment hold within it
Time's tremendous seed, all nebulae,
The sum of worlds that have been, are, and yet will be.

The writer signing off with
'happy ever after'
silences the actors
behind applause and laughter,
lowers the painted curtain
upon the play's beginning.
Goodnight. No matter whether
life or death is winning.
The characters, forever
absolved from all repining,
are only to be thought of
always intertwining
limbs on beds of roses,
endlessly at practice
of passion's pretty poses.

In Jura, where the poles are yoked together,
Tarbert's narrow but enduring tether

Neither Sound nor biting Loch can break :
And there
In love's alembic make
One out of two, and in the act prepare
An isthmus that will stand against the winter's weather.

But all who marry must
drag out a limping death
of love if they would yet
in loving draw their breath,
the moon of loving set
within the sun of lust.

In Jura, gentle island where the deer
Will scent you on the crest and turn in fear
And disappear behind the farther hill :
O then
Know that no power of will
Can track your prey down, trap it, pen
It, keep it, save by killing, pinned to now and here.

Lovers looking into
loving eyes see only
the image of their passion,
and later learn how lonely
the track that each must follow
across a desolation
of desert through the hollow
night of lunar brilliance
accompanied by that image—
until the first suspicion
of otherness is dawning,
until the recognition
of utter isolation,
the moment of decision.

In Jura, stable under moon or sun,
For all the fearful mischiefs that are done
Beyond the Sound, anxiety is not :
So let

You both without more thought
Embrace, embark, and go: the course is set:
On that high island may you love, be loved, be one.

And nothing is destroyed,
and do not fear to die,
for deep in the cold hearth
where joy's dull ashes lie
the phoenix comes to birth
and nothing is destroyed.

VI: TOWARDS THE INTERIOR

Flame on, old faithful. Fragrant wind,
Flow round me on this flowering hill.
As lizards flicker left and right
My shins brush asphodel and squill,
My fingers crush a myrtle leaf,
And potsherds crack beneath my heel.
The landscape parts and melts before
My steps that grow more urgent still.
Great Goddess, you whose breath I breathe,
Whose eye unites all good and ill,
Command, control me, free at last,
And quicken my response until
I seem to fly like Hermes held
Above the dear impeding ground
Between the twisted trembling olives
Onward, upward, towards the sound
Of light made laughter, loving
Music rooted in this holy ground.

Fabula

It had been bare for years, they said,
As good as dead, the lonely tree
Below the headland on the shore.

And sailors swore that they could hear
Above the roar of breaking seas

Its dry lament. But one dark day
(Or so they say) a flash of wings
Was seen to play about the tree,
Which put out leaves and flowers and fruit
For all to see, and like a lute

It drew such beauty from the breeze
That breaking seas were hushed and still,
So sweet the tree's new melody.

What could it be, the fishers said,
That brought the tree back from the dead?

What magic bird had sheltered there
In scented air among the boughs
Were stark and bare but yesterday?

But none could say, for none could see
Whatever lay within the tree.

Only a flash of red and gold
Was what they told me when I asked.
Both young and old had seen it flame
The day it came, the day it went,
Leaving the same old barren tree
As it had been—

                  save that its voice
Bids all rejoice and not lament.

VII: AND CROWNED WITH THE STARS

(or leaves of grass)

All who have lived now live in me
And find their concord in my veins.
This nothingness is heir to a hoard
Of treasures of a thousand reigns.
No act, no thought that's ever been thought
This earth-embracing love disdains.
Behind this breast-bone burns the sun.
Within this skull the moon gleams cold.
Ganges and Gobi I contain.
The whole Himálaya I enfold.
Darius drives across my plain,
Glitter of steel and glow of gold.
And here the far-fetched atoms meet
Where Helen and Paris lie in my limbs :
All shocks of hate and shudders of love,
All praises, curses, pleadings, hymns,
All acts of cruelty, kindness, all
Self-sacrifices, follies, crimes—
For all that has been is my demesne,
And all that I am its bounding wall,
And all that's to come must flow from me,
Both infinitely great and small
(The mere manjack being everything
Though nothing and counting for nothing at all).

Those demons, feared and honoured, may—
Can I but hold this vision tight—
Dissolve and vanish clean away
Like the trailing vapours of the night
When the sun gets up on Ida's flank
And strikes the world to life with light.

More light! More light! And still more light!

The brilliance breaks between the leaves
And spangles shady hollows where
The fighting-men unstrap their greaves,
And glances on the dancing limbs,
And out of all a pattern weaves.

Languors of steppe and soul may flow
From one poor set of fiddle-strings,
The fury of four thousand years
Rise in a wave when one voice sings,
And a slowly moving silverpoint
Spell essences of clowns and kings:
For all that is true is here and now,
And all that is past is present still:
Great Alexander lives and reigns
Forever, and there's none can kill
The tendrils that come twining, clutching,
Out of the dead around our will.

In the present moment of the past
I am a part of all that is,
And everything is part of me,
And all those Orphic melodies
That roused the rooted trees to dance
Are singing through my arteries;

And charged like the primordial sun
With power of total density
(And still without an inward sign,
Our outward, of finality),
I tremble to discharge this joy
Like showers of gold on Danaë.

Cleopatra, Helen, Grainné,
She whose hair has trapped the rays,
One woman yet all women, she
At the sacred centre of the maze—
Let the bridge towards her bear
The traffic of a thousand million days.

Kissed in the park, she cried

The gothick tower clapped out the skinny hour
Across the shipyards and the housing-schemes
And Ferry Green where suddenly a shower
Washed out the old men from their distant dreams.

Like sponges, all those Works—released and squeezed
At stated hours, absorbing and expelling
The tamed floods of life.
                      But the Regal teased
The dulled desires into a torrent, welling
Up to the screen, and later gilding the grimy
Streets.
            Kissed in the park, she cried: 'May I
Too shake these shackles off, so cold, so slimy,
And sway a million with a smile or sigh!'

Duologue

I love you. What did you expect?
—Not that it would be like this.
And how else should it be?
—There was a strangeness in your kiss:
  You were not kissing me.

          He sighed, and so did she.

I love you. Isn't that enough?
—I do not know whose lips you kissed.
In any glass you'd see.
—Well, tell me what it was I missed
  So agonisingly.

          He stirred, and so did she.

I love you for yourself alone.
—It wasn't I whom you caressed.
It was, and lovingly.

—The woman loved is truly blest
And knows it instantly.

He frowned, and so did she.

I love you. Must you ask for proof?
—You love an image of desire.
Such words are lost on me.
—My lips mere fuel for a fire
Kindled by fantasy.

He rose, and so did she.

VIII: OF OTHER DAYS

Inexorable, innocent,
The wind and tide ran hand in hand,
And eager fingers rose and fell
And came again upon the sand,
Leaving for me a line of longing
Looped along the flank of land;

And once I leant upon a wind
Of liquid diamond on a crest,
Nostrils flared, face seared, and eyes
Half-closed against the flaming west
Where looming coolins from my depths
A sweet and siren poison pressed;

And once at the ebb of day by a tangled
Shore a distant piper drew
A silver zero in the sky
And pulled my very being through
The lips of nothingness until
It bled into the dwindling blue;

The power that pulls the needle round
Pulled me also: between the larch
I tracked the wraiths I'd loosed to lure me
Over the taiga on a march
That left me at the bitter end
Cold as the Pole and stiff as starch;

How many times I ran with rain
Down Glasgow gutters, soared with sheets
Of newsprint in Third Avenue,
In Stockholm cracked beneath careless feet
Like early ice, in London flowed
With November mist down a Fulham street,
And stretched by the Brandenburger gate

With a shard of bleached and broken bone,
In Paris poured myself with piss
Or pastis over zinc or stone,
And from the Hill of Howth dissolved
And drowned into the Bailey's groan!

As if on a backward-running reel
The images of life went helter-
Skelter off to vanishing point.
The shivering self, deprived of shelter,
Dried like a spittle in the wind
And disappeared into the welter.

All into nothing, again and again,
And yet not once was there any lack
Of love within (for love's the word),
And now that load is off my back,
Assured of plenty I proclaim:
The more goes out, the more comes back.

The ash I've mumbled on my tongue
So long has kept my palate clean;
The haze I've held before my eyes
Has honed my vision razor-keen:
Not even old Van Winkle sighing,
Waking, wondering, welcomed such a scene.

Prayer for a sentry
(after Permeke)

Not strong, not tall,
a stone at his heart,
yet he stands like a wall
in his lumpish boots.
He is limbed like a doll
in pathos of lead,
yet his life is a feather,

whose face is rough
with beer and weather.
A stone's at his heart
yet his heart is not stone,
who stands alone
in lumpish boots
in pathos of lead.
At the distant end
he stands like a wall
upon many dead.
Tender his roots
though rough his head,
who stands like a wall
at the end of the garden.
Frost, do not harden
him. Sun, ascend.
And today let fall,
impassive God
of soul and clod,
no jagged rain,
no shower of pain
upon that head.

Pale dust on a narrow lane

Pale dust on a narrow lane lapped by the foam of hawthorn.
A pond gleamed beside it and tall elms leant across it,
Twining their arms together, and larks from a distant dazzle
Quickened the air as he walked.

For there in the springtime he walked, and as though spring were
forever,
And the pale lane had no ending, and the elms would always be
budding,
And the larks from the dazzle singing, and the hedges creaming
and scented.
An unseen corner drew near.

Now that long-seen corners draw nearer, he thinks of the dust
    and the gleam of
The pond, and the elms and the hawthorn, the tremulous air
    and larks singing,
Of the girl whose hair was like sunshine, and he utters these
    words like one stricken :
Pale dust on a narrow lane.

Midsummer night's dream

Because it is Midsummer Night
and now that everything is still
he summons to his inward sight
the dusty road, the swooping hill,
the winking Hebridean light
beyond Argyll, the hidden stone
he stumbled on—and finds himself alone.

For every abstract fury was ready for the kill.

Ten years ago they climbed that hill
and walked the ridge-road through the night.
The land of Cowal was lying still
beneath a milky flood of light,
and silent was their march until
the clatter of that tumbling stone
roused half the sleeping dogs from Kames to Strone.

And every abstract fury was circling like a kite.

'A mhuirnín, here's Midsummer Night—
and do you not remember still
that climb from Glendaruel, the sight
of mist upon the highest hill,
the dogs' alarm, the flashing light
beyond Argyll, the hidden stone
I stumbled on ? But no, I am alone.'

For every abstract fury was ready for the kill.

While lapdogs cock

While lapdogs cock their dandy legs
and old men mumble in their snooze,
pale dust puffs out from underfoot
and heat lies thick like layers of ooze.

A lumpish infant's lollipop
makes sticky dribble. Infant smears
cross Mummy's naked sun-blotched legs—
an incident that leads to tears.

But see Mum's pleasure in those youngsters
leaping from bounding board and spangling
shimmering quivering air with showering
rainbow fragments coldly jangling
between the pool and the sun's hot glowering!

Awnings stretch their sugar-stripes
and mask with a brow-easing light
the sweetly sheltered place beneath
where girls and Gordons wait for night,
the velvet and impassive dark
which tolerates the pitch-and-toss
and scuffle in the scrubby park.

A mile above this barbéd coast
five hundred boys drone through the air
to seek another bristling beach
and scatter metal petals there;
and lapdogs cock their dandy legs,
and gaffers grumble in their nap,
and dust puffs out from underfoot,
and Calum's got a dose of clap.

Far from familiar waters

Far from familiar waters and the long lift of the hills
And the taut curve of the leaping fish and the screaming reel
And the wind round Vorlich's shoulder, soft wind from
   Lochgoilhead,
The township lapped in your love:
So far, Colin, from these, how many horizons dividing,
And far from the dwindling trees of Tarbet, the twining tracks
And the black bitten rocks above Arrochar, far, so far,
And far from the narrow loch;
The flowers of Ardgartan's forest and foreland, far from these,
And far from the tangled shore where the lanky heron is fishing,
The belling of stags in mist, the drowsy drift of myrtle,
Allt a' Bhalachain's rush and the hush in the air at evening,
Far from all these
Your death.

But under the vulture sun, Colin, gentlest of all of us,
Deep in the deadly fight, did the warpipes' screaming torrent
Strike from the sand as you fell your own true habitation,
Conjuring pine and birch,
Before the darkness, cold as the depths of Loch Long and darker,
Welling within you and surging darkly upward and over
Your vision, dissolved all images into irrelevance,
Acquiescence,
Death?

Now I recall you as I knew you first:
Withdrawn, yet not a solitary man;
Fine as the Spanish steel your people wore
Three centuries ago in simpler wars
(Bent point to pommel, yet they would not snap),
And innocent of hatred as the wind.

You were the best among us, you who marched
Beside your piper, looking round and smiling,
So far from her was love was all your dreaming,
To meet the shot that gave your life its meaning.

Your twenty-second year was scarcely out
When one small patch of sand drank down your blood,
Yet I shall never think of you abandoned,
Nor as rejected like a sculptor's clay
Before the inner truth has shaped the skin,
But both as man and mystery of fulfilment:
The circle closed, all longing satisfied.

Scarface and sceptic

Scarface and sceptic, Campbell, long years dead,
Tell me the words that would not make you throw
Your long head back and mock me like a crow.

'Well, once in Furness, pausing on a crest,
I turned, a blankness in my eyes, and said:
"We leave tomorrow morning, and I know . . ." '

And so did I know, Michael, what the rest
Would be, even as you laughed and mocked your thought,
My silence, and the whole envenomed world.

Into the howling maelstrom you were hurled,
Laughing to learn that laughter's at the core
Of terror, knowing well (as I did not)
That when the flag of lunacy's unfurled
You meet the banner-man with mocking roar.

And so you met him, fifty miles from Rome.

And so I set it down, who stayed at home.

No wind in Glendaloch

No wind in Glendaloch that glinting day
When spring drove into winter its bright wedge
And the young sun tried its strength upon the gray
Stones, touching the trees around the lake's edge,
While the stream chattered love (their love alone,
All else shut out).

              But when he called the saint,
Old Kevin turned her ankle on a stone,
Finding in human love inhuman taint.

Wry saint, goodbye.
              From Laragh, to the hills.
A bitter gale there under a clear sky
As bright as quattrocento distance. Rills
Frayed out in falling scarves to catch her eye.

How bittersweet the love, how taut the strain.

At the crossroads they paused. Which way to go?
How could they tell, engulfed in love and pain,
Happy and hopeless, whatever could they know,
Clinging through a mist of kisses and tears,
But that black night must come when she must leave—
And, forced apart by hopes and miles and fears,
In London she, in Dublin he would grieve?

At last he said, 'That way!'—forward or back,
The right road or the wrong, he did not care—
And watched her as she drove the winding track,
And wondered why such beauty bred despair:
Beauty of hill and flesh and sky and bone
Framed in the window of the rented Ford.

'Dear Christ, to have it for myself alone
All Ireland might be put to fire and sword.
Joy I had known like any, deep loss too,
But on that hill-pass high above Loch Tay,
In company with fire and ice and you,
I learned love's anguish no glib words can say.'

'*A child*—so *high* . . . '

> 'Tree you are,
> Moss you are,
> You are violets with wind above them.
> A child—*so* high—you are
> And all this is folly to the world.'
>   —Ezra Pound : *A Girl*

Which proves the world's perennial folly
to one who knows a birch-tree in her grace
and in her tenderness the touch of moss,
violets in her breath, and in
her candour a child—*so* high—
and knows that none of this is folly
but, au contraire, a wisdom such
as could not be divined
by any yob who passed them on a bench
in sunshine outside a pub—
how could he know that the long man and the girl in black jeans
were deep in a mossy birch-wood
on a bank of violets with wind above them,
far from the Builders' Arms,
remote from the folly of the world?

Stale gravity to daunce
(a Gaelic metre imitated)

'Now let me praise her
who haunts all my evenings,
and evil on him
whose harsh voice disturbs me.

I'll let none disturb me
or draw me away
from wild wayward sweetness
and sadness of dreams.

37

What have I but dreams
to delight me alone here,
and hopes that they shall
all be shared by my darling?

In sleep she'll cry, 'Darling!'
my dear one, my life,
our lips and our limbs met,
no matter the miles

between us, the miles
one morning will vanquish.
In vain till then pine.
To please me I'll praise her

and praise her and praise her
who haunts all my evenings,
and evil on him
whose harsh voice disturbs me.'

IX: THE BOUNTY OF GOD

The town was taken.
                Alasdair
Mac Cholla Chiotach and his men
Of Ulster and the Isles were loosed
Upon the streets of Aberdeen—
Ten such days and ten such nights
Would make a moment where I've been.

Flowers of citrus shake their scent
Across the frenzied play below,
And cool the flakes of sunlight falling
Over all from top to toe,
While the singers and the dancers all
Move rhythmically to and fro.

When the mirror of malicious eyes
Is cracked at last, a man may either
Cease to exist or find himself
No longer through the eyes of another.
Knowing himself, he knows the world
Is his, and would not envy God the Father.

Casualty report

He left the tiresome party, turned into the hall,
And there she was, with no one else around.
'Dear girl,' he said, and kissed her cheek, and that was all
Until he looked into her eyes and drowned.

The tall chrysanthemums

The tall chrysanthemums
are drooping now, and now
the dark is still a toy
eyes have not tired of yet:
but how should we forget
the summer's mounting joy,
or in late autumn how
eyes drank chrysanthemums?

Et cetera (see Roget)

'My young love, my late love,
my dear one, my darling,
the grace of your gesture
had wounded me sorely
before your sweet half-smile
disarmed me entirely.'

Poor fool, to begin with
he'd thought, 'Take love easy!'
as if their first kiss had
not made him her captive.
But now he'll confess it:

'Enchained and transported,
besotted, bewildered,
enraptured and ravished,
bemused and bedazzled,
entranced and enchanted,
et cetera (see *Roget*)—
and unfit for rhyming
on Valentine's morning.'

Her beauty had filled all
his being with longing
and loving and hoping

and praising and fearing,
lamenting the lost years
of past and of future—
but most with rejoicing
that ever he met his
sweet marvel and mistress,
his young love, his late love,
his dear one, his darling.

Pillowtalk

'I am not beautiful,' she'll say,
'Just ordinary in every way.'
—Just so the dawning of each common day.

'You are besotted, I suppose,
But why with me, Lord only knows.'
—But ask His Lordship why he made the rose.

Leaving her, still

Leaving her, still with the freshness of her sound, touch, taste, and
  sight
On every sense,
The indescribable delight
Of what they made together in the night,
And, even more, that tenderness
Of total lovingness
When two apart are still more one than two-made-one,
Buoyed him into the air away from her,
Watching the Boeing from the window,
Yet with him still.

X: VALE ATQUE AVE

To be plunged into pleasure as an arm
Is plunged in a glowing mound of grain,
While the flask is tilted and the wine
Runs rosy, trickling from the chin,
And the flesh, like ground to green fingers,
Quickens with life, awaits the rain . . .

And a small rain from the sea drifts in
To blur those images.
     A breath
Stirs in the pine.
     The peepshow dulls
To darkness.
    In the rocks beneath
The cliff-edge swings the wave.
       The light's
Been dowsed.
    The bell is silent.
      Death
Of a small sort drains the moment dry.
But through the huge and hollow night
Whispers a voice :
    'Rejoice!'
      A wind
In the pine ?
   The tide ?
      I turn away
And smile to see the steady lamp
Beside the walls that once housed Valéry.

Time was

(variations on a theme of Anthony Raftery's)

Time was when he turned in he was at home.
No longer. To himself he's now a stranger.
Where once he wandered wealthy among marvels—
Blank walls only, enclosing only blankness.
—'Gone my delight, gone too the glint of danger,
Gone all that grace as radiant as Rome,
And gone the fear of loss that forced bright marvels
Out of the dark. Now all that's left is blankness.'

Time was when fear of loss fed his delight.
No longer. Hope's long dying drained him hollow.
Where once he wandered cherishing his anguish—
Vacancy unfolding into vacancy.
—'Pain once sustained me when I could not follow
Her, anguish when she wasn't in my sight.
Christ, fill this blankness with returning anguish,
Flood with fresh pain these plains of vacancy!'

By Loch Tay in the mountains

(variations on an Irish air)

Once on a time
by Loch Tay in the mountains
the tall grass
was shaking,
and I, come to climb
to the crest of the mountains,
the heart in
me breaking,
stood still for a time
by Loch Tay in the mountains.

Sadly I stood
by the brink of the water,

my eyes on
the hillside,
but quickly my blood
ran as wild as the water
that broke in
a white tide
below where I stood
by the brink of the water.

I was alone
like the strange one was singing
and crossing the heather:
the heart that was stone
came to life at her singing,
and coming
together,
we two were alone
as the hill-wind was singing.

Dead leaves were burned
by Loch Tay in the mountains
that morning
together,
for then, love, I learned
love is not like the mountains
but frail as
a feather
or faded leaves burned
by Loch Tay in the mountains.

EPILOGUE

Mary Stewart's admonition
(en ma fin est mon commencement)

Why do you weep ? Why do you grieve ?
Death and decay are my beginning.
Birth and growth and death but weave
A tapestry from lifelines spinning
Endlessly, the lines whose end
Cannot be told from their beginning.

Why grieve at winter, friends, why weep ?
To wake, the world must also sleep.

Why do you weep ? Why do you grieve
For one who finds her life beginning
Ever anew as minutes weave
A tapestry from lifelines spinning,
Knowing that what is known as end
Can't be unstitched from its beginning ?

The morning after

Before the cloth and the paint
The pattern's realised,
And hero, fool, and saint
Are plainly recognised.

The swinging nebulae,
Their rhythm understood,
Resolve within the blood
Their contrapuntal play.

Grease and powder and hair
And cunning voice contrive

The toppling tower of Lear
Till every jack alive
Drowns in a sea of sorrow.

Yet Comedy's the wall
We'll climb upon tomorrow,
Smiling at it all.

The one way to get
To the land of Et-Et
Is round and about
Through the maze of Aut-Aut.